WHERE DID IT COME FROM?

# INVENTING THE BICYCLE

I0802822

by Emma Carlson Berne

Consultant: Beth Gambro
Reading Specialist, Yorkville, Illinois

BEARPORT PUBLISHING

Bearcub Books, an imprint of Bearport Publishing by FlutterBee

# Teaching Tips

## Before Reading

- Look at the cover of the book. Discuss the picture and the title.
- Ask readers to brainstorm a list of what they already know about bicycles. What can they expect to see in the book?
- Go on a picture walk, looking through the pictures to discuss vocabulary and make predictions about the text.

## During Reading

- Read for purpose. Encourage readers to think about what led to the creation of the bicycle as they are reading.
- Ask readers to look for the details of the book. How was the first bicycle different from bicycles today?
- If readers encounter an unknown word, ask them to look at the sounds in the word. Then, ask them to look at the rest of the page. Are there any clues to help them understand?

## After Reading

- Encourage readers to pick a buddy and reread the book together.
- Ask readers to name two things that happened as the bicycle was being invented. Find the pages that tell about these things.
- Ask readers to write or draw something they learned about bicycles.

**Credits**
Cover and title page, © shcherbak volodymyr/iStock; 3, © skodonnell/iStock; 5, © Somkid Saowaros/Shutterstock; 7, © CasarsaGuru/iStock; 9, © Pictorial Press Ltd/Alamy Stock Photo; 11, © Public Domain/Wikimedia Commons; 13, © Photo Josse/Leemage/Getty Images; 15, © Science & Society Picture Library/Getty Images; 17, © Zuri Swimmer /Alamy Stock Photo; 19, © isabella antonelli/iStock; 21, © Sergey Novikov/Shutterstock; 22T, © Douglas Miller/ Getty Images; 22M, © pixinoo/Shutterstock; 22B, © Duncan Andison/Shutterstock; 23TL, © Gargantiopa/Shutterstock; 23TR, © Vladyslav Starozhylov/Shutterstock; 23BL, © MIND AND I/Shutterstock; 23BR, © PeopleImages.com - Yuri A/ Shutterstock.

See BearportPublishing.com for our statement on Generative AI Usage.

Library of Congress Cataloging-in-Publication Data is available at www.loc.gov or upon request from the publisher.

ISBN: 979-8-89577-586-8 (hardcover)
ISBN: 979-8-89577-766-4 (paperback)
ISBN: 979-8-89577-674-2 (ebook)

Copyright © 2026 Bearport Publishing Company. All rights reserved. No part of this publication may be reproduced in whole or in part, stored in any retrieval system, or transmitted in any form or by any means, electronic, mechanical, photocopying, recording, or otherwise, without written permission from the publisher. Bearport Publishing is a division of FlutterBee Education Group.

For more information, write to Bearport Publishing, 3500 American Blvd W, Suite 150, Bloomington, MN 55431.
Printed in the United States of America.

# Contents

# Zoom!

Get on your bicycle.

Let's go for a ride!

Bikes are a fast way to get around.

But where did they come from?

Before bicycles, many people walked.

Some rode horses.

But horses were hard to take care of.

People needed another way to get around.

Karl von Drais had the answer.

He **invented** a machine with four wheels.

The machine was very big.

It needed two people to make it move.

Karl von Drais

In 1817, he made another machine.

This one had a wood **frame** and two wheels.

This early bike was called a velocipede.

**Say velocipede like vuh-LAH-si-*peed***

A person pushed off on the ground.

The handles turned the front wheel.

Then, the velocipede turned.

This was faster than walking.

But the bike did not have **brakes**.

People had to use their feet to stop.

People around the world liked the velocipede.

Some people raced to see who could go fastest.

James Moore won the first race.

James
Moore

Later, people added **pedals**.

These helped move the wheels.

This made bikes even easier to ride.

A pedal

Bikes can take us almost anywhere.

Some people ride to work.

Others zoom around for fun.

Let's go for a ride!

# Fun Bike Facts

The longest bicycle in the world fits more than 30 riders!

Early bikes were very bumpy to ride. People called them bone-shakers.

The best bikers can go faster than most cars.

# Glossary

**brakes** parts of vehicles that help them slow down or stop

**frame** a structure that supports something

**invented** created for the first time

**pedals** foot levers used to make bikes go

# Index



# Read More

**Coupe, Jessica.** *Bicycling (Like a Pro).* New York: Lightbox Learning Inc., 2023.

**Owings, Lisa.** *Biking (Blastoff! Readers Level 2: Let's Get Outdoors).* Minneapolis: Bellwether Media, 2023.

# Learn More Online

1. Go to **FactSurfer.com** or scan the QR code below.
2. Enter "**Inventing the Bicycle**" into the search box.
3. Click on the cover of this book to see a list of websites.

# About the Author

Emma Carlson Berne is the author of many books. She lives in Cincinnati, Ohio, with her husband, three children, one grumpy cat, and one friendly cat.